South Carolina Bards Poetry Anthology

2024

Edited by
James P. Wagner (Ishwa)

South Carolina Bards Poetry Anthology

Copyright © 2024 by LG Press

www.localgemspoetrypress.com

All rights reserved. No part of this book may be reproduced or transmitted in any form or by any means without written permission of the authors.

Table of Contents

Megan Alexander 1
Justin Shaun Anderson 4
Pathronda Anderson 6
Shelia L. Anderson 8
Paula Appling 10
Danny P. Barbare 11
Camryn Barnhart 12
Roland Wayne Bebler 13
A. C. Blake 14
Richard Bowerman 16
Piper Brinkley 18
William Jefferson Bryson Jr. 21
Alyssa Campbell 23
James Campbell 25
Kira Carman 27
Debbie De Louise 28
Mackenzie Doherty 31
Matthew Eastland 33
Caroline Eastman 35
Bill Egan 37
Carley Eason Evans 39
Angela Feathers 41
Jayne Jaudon Ferrer 43

Jennifer J. Foreman 45
Renee Gahan 47
Jessica Gent 49
Beverly George 51
Meta m Griffin 53
Sam Harrelson 55
Michael Hill 57
Robert W. Hill 59
Jared Hove 61
Laura Howard 63
Madi Huffman 65
Debbie Hutchinson 67
Lucas James 69
David Rhoades Johnson 71
Jerry T. Johnson 73
Debi Jones 75
Kimberly June 76
Renee Kalagayan 78
Brittany Kay 80
Rebecca Martin Kraus 82
Riley Legette 84
Faith Litchfield 86
Kathryn Etters Lovatt 88
Angela Mason Lowe 90
Neil MacAulay 92
Natalie Malone 93

Robert Matheson	95
Elaine Mathis	96
Elmore McLeod	98
Samantha McLeod	101
Catelyn Cecile Meeker	103
Stacey Militana	105
Connie L. Montgomery	107
Susan Mouw	108
Emily O'Neil	110
Gene Owens	112
Tony Owens	114
Tolar Parker	116
Jessica Rainey	118
Arthurine Rice	120
LaToya Richburg	122
Jim R. Rogers	124
Ron Roth	126
August Sage	128
Joanna Schuman	130
Patricia Shea	132
Peggy Shrum	135
Amanda Britton Smith	138
Angela Thomas Smith	139
Jeff Snyder	141
Wendy Soltis	142
Tyler Spencer	144

Melissa Whiteford St. Clair 146
Halie Stockett 148
HollyAnna Vaughn 150
Christine Vernon 152
Richard Wainright 153
Marv Ward 156
Amanda Rachelle Warren 157
Riley Willis 159
Leslie Harper Worthington 160
Toretha Wright 162

Megan Alexander

Holy

A queen knows her holy ground. *Am I supposed to be holy?*

Your face within the paint covering the thin walls
Bloody handprints on the broken door
Your voice as the wooden floorboards creak
The door doesn't lock
Your dull eyes watching me through the mirrors
Everything has shattered.
I was always talking to the wrong mirrors.

How could I let this happen?
*What **is** happening?*
How can I fix this?
Can I fix this?

Holy, Holy, Holy

My screams, her tears, *your silence*
Your silence, her blood, my tears
My blood, her screams, *your silence*
Silence, silence, silence,
 please,

As the broken record plays
Perpetually on repeat

Again, again, *again*
I'll do better, it won't happen again
I'll save us.

I gave you everything I owned
I let you build my home
I loved you with everything I had,
 But you, you were the monster
You craved destruction,
Sinister, righteous, demonic, holy
Patient, loving, kind,
Obsessive, manipulative, **liar**,
Holy, holy, holy,

Under the bed, in the kitchen,
In the closet, on the couch
On the patio, in the car,
At work, at home,
Nowhere, everywhere and everything in between.

Holy, Holy, Holy

How long will this last?
How long has it been?
Only two more years to go?
It's almost over.
It will never end.

You still haunt my mind,
Dull eyes and haunting smile
Im gasping for air,

You are following me,
I can't sleep ,
You are following me
You're at the door, **knock knock**,
Following me,
Making it known you're still waiting for me to come back.

Holy, holy, ho–

I *won't* go back
I *will* look for you
I *don't* want you here
I *do* miss you

For the record, I was the record
You broke it,
You played it,
You loved me, You broke me.

Megan Alexander is 24 years old and was born and raised in South Carolina. She moved away at the age of 20 to the midwest to see what it was like in another place besides her hometown. While away, she grew a love for the fast city but ended up coming back to her hometown after only two years. She developed a love for poetry while away, but has never gained the courage to write until now.

Justin Shaun Anderson

Naked Coffee

His words were spoke in whispers
Over whisps of heat yes steam
He uttered a moan that drew me
In further from my daydream
Who wants two Fraps alone
He sighed staring at the menu
Of mixes that would make his drink his own
What's so wrong with naked coffee
Basic is better.
The sinful hint of nut makes it so robust
Wetting my palette and taste it
I don't need whipped cream, caramel, sprinkles, trust
Maybe I'm old fashioned. Better balanced by my bitter drink.
There's way too many options for me to bear to think.
My coffee called. Just basic and black
I nodded and he looked up and grinned.
See yes. Amen
He leaned closer. Became bolder
And asked to be my friend
For his favorite time for coffee was now when night began
I interjected decaff I need without the yellow sugar he agreed
I do fancy dear fella occasionally
A bit of a twist with a French vanilla
From six to nine is a great time to be good to the last drop
We sat and drank til the clock chimed to stop

I saddened for us to part as I put my mug away
He walked up and grinned
Maybe, he wondered, we could talk about coffee and other things in the night again

---

He is an English teacher who helps change the world by helping students tap into their own creativity. He loves to write poetry and short stories. He predominantly writes about queer and Black love.

Pathronda Anderson

Death of the dawn

Anything that has life on earth is meant to die one day and those who are left behind will cry tears of loneliness and grief and feel like they will never recover from the loss.
The tears of rain from feeling sad and alone may sometimes seem to last for a lifetime but, in time it will get better but, not forgotten.
The flesh of skin that surrounds the skeleton of the body will eventually rot away and leave skeletal bones dried and brittle as it turns into dust because ashes to ashes and dust to dust.
Death of the dawn has its own time and place, so we need to get ourselves in order with things we have done here on Earth so when it is our time to go, we will not be afraid .
We do not know when, where, how, why and time because we could go at any time of the day or night, so we need our souls to be right and to seek Jesus's face as we continue to run the final race .
Death of the dawn is surely coming soon so make no mistake about this because we are not meant to stay here forever.
Death angel is cruising down every street corner driving the Cadilac of darkness on his evil highway , and he loves to cause gloom of accidents filled with death.
Death of the dawn has no morals or anything that is good and peaceful but, there is a happier place that is waiting for you and I and that is a place beyond the skies of blue and the fluffy clouds of white that is called heaven and there is a beauty of a garden where roses of different colors and fragrances will live forever.

Pathronda is a very creative person and she is also legally blind because she was born with Retinitis Pigmentosa.

Shelia L. Anderson

The Swing

An elusive autumn breeze
Gently pushed a swing
That hung from an ancient oak.
Fashioned by a proud father
For his only son,
Hopeful that he would soon share it.
Only now, the swing sits empty—
Abandoned.
The promise of another son
Was suddenly, painfully lost.
Born too soon--
And then gone.
It proved too much—
The pain of it all.
Both he and she together
Were not enough.
Neither could find the strength
To push away the pain,
To soothe the other's hurt and aching heart.
So, the house and yard sit lifeless,
And the swing remains empty—motionless—
Except for an elusive autumn breeze
That gives it a gentle push.

Shelia L. Anderson, a retired educator, is a native of Charleston, South Carolina. Anderson earned a Bachelor's degree in English from Winthrop College and a Master's degree in English from The Citadel. Anderson has published ten books, including five children's books. She continues to teach part time as a substitute teacher. She also leads a Bible study group. In addition to reading and writing, she enjoys gardening. Anderson has three grown children, four grandchildren and one great-grandson.

Paula Appling

D. punctatus

Salmon bellied, balled-up coil
suns itself on sandy soil
too obvious to be missed.

Pewter-colored with grey neck ring
A month old now, hatched in spring.
Captured and unhappy. Tries to resist.

Reptile brain said fight or flight
It jabbed me with a tiny strike
Its message clear: desist!

I freed the seven-inch-long snake
And hoped he pardoned my mistake
But know! Brazen humans will persist.

Paula Appling is an editor and emerging poet from the east coast, currently hanging her hat in upstate South Carolina. Inspired by nature and life itself, she writes about the wonder, love, and mystery in our experiences. When she's not chasing the elusive rhyme, she's hoping to spot the white tipped tail of a red fox on the trail.

Danny P. Barbare

The Apple Orchard

Apples, a carnival, people like bees that buzz about—a
bushel, a peck,--
cider,
funnel cake, clover honey, peppermint
jelly,
scuppernong, white
lightning, chow chow mild or hot, corn
relish,
and other
bottles of goods for a sweet seasonal winter down South.

Danny P. Barbare resides in Greenville, SC. His poetry has appeared locally and abroad. He says he loves to travel to the Blue Ridge and the lowlands of Charleston, SC. He lives with his wife in Greenville.

Camryn Barnhart

Frankie's Fun Park
Run down paradise
For sun-bleached mini golf dates
Cheap snacks, and go-karts

Carolina Rain
Carolina rain -
Like rinsin' a red-hot pan,
makes sizzling sidewalks.

Folly Washout
Sand scorches red feet
My graffiti odyssey
Gifts me a lighthouse

Camryn is a poet from Charleston, South Carolina. She is a graduate of the College of Charleston, and often visits Folly Beach with her beloved border collie, Margot. She feels conflicted about where she's from in many ways, but is grateful to live in such a beautiful place, often finding inspiration in the region's unique culture and scenery.

Roland Wayne Bebler

September

It bloomed with so much hope
In the spring
Like early flowers
Giving birth to dreams
And grew intensely passionately
Though the summer months
Now brutal bitter assassinating
Late autumn winds
Whip heart bare trees
That cried their last tears in October
Over the September death of
Our summer love

Roland Wayne Bebler grew up in New Jersey but has lived around the country including the San Francisco area and the Carolinas. He has seen some of his poetry published in some anthologies. He is currently trying to but together some of his poems for a book publication.

A. C. Blake

Do Little Field

Hundreds of private airports,
Scattered throughout the state,
 Airplane hangars like garages,
On houses by the gate.

The Sunday Breakfast Club,
 Greets planes for breakfast fare,
Experimental models,
Two-seaters in the air.

Four-seaters, restored classics,
 Life on a private airstrip,
Surrounded by scrub oaks and swamps,
Grass runway, a peaceful trip.

Restored MGs escort pilots,
 To and from the breakfast meet,
 In one of the empty hangars,
Where community and pilots greet.

Quickie Q2, dragonfly grace,
 My husband's pride and delight,
 His quonset hangar, self-built space,
In this shared hobby, our spirits take flight.

Do Little Field in South Carolina,
Hosts a breakfast fly-in scene,
The fun and joy of flying,
In this cherished airstrip dream.

Anne Catharine Blake is a freelance author and illustrator whose works are deeply influenced by her Canadian and Southern American heritage, infusing them with both humor and cultural richness. Her illustrated books, poems, and stories have garnered international acclaim and have been published and exhibited extensively.

Richard Bowerman

Ode to the Marlow Brothers

(Charles, Alfred, Boone, George, and Lewellyn)

In the annals of the Old West, as this incredible true story goes,
lived a good and proud family, known as the nomad Marlows.
Doctor Marlow raised a family in a town that would bear his name,
the fate that would befall four of his sons, was such a crying shame!

The brothers where no angels, though never broke the law to any degree,
although one brother killed a man in self-defense and got a reprieve.
The local Marshal "had it in" for the brothers and to see them gone,
so, he had them arrested for stealing horses, which was totally-wrong!

The Marshal and his Deputies then incited the town into an angry mob,
so, he had to move the prisoners, and hired some guards to do the job.
Then off to a Texas trial in a wagon went the brothers, shackled to one another, the Marshals and mob hid in ambush and opened fire as the boys dove for cover

The brothers returned fire with guns taken from the guards, as they ran,

the firefight was so fierce, there was blood spilled, by most every man.
Two brothers died and the other two, while wounded, drove off the mob,
then they freed their shackles and escaped in the wagon, thru the smokey fog.

Federal Judge McCormick ask about the overdue Marlow brothers,
his honor was told of the ambush by the Marshals and many others.
The Judge reviewed and ruled to exonerate the Marlow brothers
and said bring me those in the ambush, the law will make them suffer!

The two severally wounded Marlow brothers survived and started a new life,
they each moved to Colorado and lived with their children and their wife.
Several years passed for the guilty to be brought to trial, to no one's glory.
 The Judge stated "their courage should be commemorated in song and story!"

Since retiring and moving to the Carolinas 7 years ago with his wife, Richard has enjoyed a new life style. Warmer weather has allowed for year-round golf, more affordable cost of living and Richard has even become an avid gardener and a South Carolina history buff. His love of poetry prevails and he has written several poems recently including, poems presented to the South Carolina Bards Poetry Anthology 2021 and 2022.

Piper Brinkley

The Piper

everyone pays the piper
and I'm collecting my due
if I choose you
it's not nothing
you only owe me everything
you can pay in love
in affection, effort
in bravery, with pleasure
with focus and attention
with vulnerability
in space, in time

everyone pays the piper
follow me you'll see
you either pay in love
or longing, or regret
you'll pay in sorrow
with your debts
you'll pay in loss because
everyone pays the piper
so pay up in the up and up
don't realize too late
what you'll really have to owe

I decide, it's up to me
what is to be indebted
I've taken the payments of fools
paying in their sadness
in guilt, in karma
in cowardness
in painful deprivation
everyone pays the piper
and I'm collecting my due

each payment adds to my melody
my strength to attune
it richens my very tone
builds my trilling power
my breath unending
a perpetual piper
a snake swallowing its tail

I whistle my tune
that perks the ears
of those
only meant to hear
if I stir in you a need to dance
come follow me
and you'll see

everyone pays the piper
and most willingly
for the offspring of joy
from your love tokens paid
come back to you
my love the reward

with each deposit
the descendants
of our love
will be safe
precious moments that ring
bright and true
multiplying our brood in tune

if I choose you
it's not nothing
you only owe me everything
I don't feel sorry
you have been warned
for eons, it's been whispered
everyone pays the piper
and now I'm collecting my due

Piper Brinkley is a mother, poet, author, Divorce Doula and Transitions Coach, Certified Divorce Coach. She is a lifelong health, wellness, and happiness advocate. Her passion is to empower women to shine after being shattered and to guide them to rediscover their personal power through prose, humor, and perspective shifts.

William Jefferson Bryson Jr.

Among My Mother's Things

Among my mother's things
Are things I have left
As she left them
Because they were hers
And she is gone.

Long time gone, now
And I am what is left
To leave these things
As she left them
Or not.

I will myself soon enough be leaving
And there will be no one else
To leave these things
As she left them
Or not.

Among my mother's things
A small ladies' travel trunk
From an earlier era, her mother's
Once an item of necessity
Of import
Full, now, only
Of what the mice have left

Of my ancestors.

They live on thin, foxed, fragile paper
In my mother's hand
And in her mother's hand
Or in pieces
In disintegrating newspaper clippings
Of obituaries
Of birth notices
Of marriages
Of military discharges
Of achievements and recognitions and awards

Their remnants stuck to pages
And pieces of pages, loose now
Once in scrapbooks
What covers they had
And the binding
That held them together
That held everything together
Gone forever
Lost in time.

William Jefferson Bryson Jr. describes himself as a retired Social Worker. He served as South Carolina's State Ombudsman from 1987 to 1999. He writes poetry to help him make sense of the world, and of himself.

Alyssa Campbell

Hybridization

Cohen states monsters are hybrids.

What am I but a hybrid?
I am neither this nor that.
I belong neither here nor there.
Am I a monster?
Will I be told as one?

I feel as though I am a flag,
being batted back-and-forth in the wind.
I feel as though I am a garment,
being worn for an occasion then given away.
I feel as though I am a lost hero questless,
not as the tale's monster.

Is it my fault I am a hybrid?
Is it my fault I am unclaimed?
Is it my fault I am passed around?

I am a creation of those loving and neglecting me.
I am a creation of unwantedness.
I am but a hybrid.

Alyssa Campbell is attending Lander University and working on a Bachelors in Professional Writing. She runs a creative website, Campbell Curiosities, with her sisters and mother and is working on self-publishing a poetry book through B&N Press with the date to be announced.

James Campbell

Open Gate

Just outside the city
Past the old train tracks
There is an iron gate
Standing open, painted black.
A low stone and mossy wall
Runs along the tree-lined road
Around a quiet, peaceful place
Where I sometimes go.
At times in the evening
I walk among the stones
And ponder the departed
As I walk the path alone.
I pause to read the epitaphs-
Lives brought down to a line.
I wonder about their lives
And those they left behind.
I walk beneath the shade
Of the cemetery trees,
The dappled sunlight dancing
Where it passes through the leaves.
Hundreds of lives that have passed
Hundreds of lives now gone,
Most no living eye has seen,
Most no living soul has known.
Centuries of memories

Echo softly in this place,
And I am drawn here to walk
With the sun upon my face
Until one day in the future
My name is etched in stone
And there's a quiet epitaph
That is my very own.
Then for the final time
I will make my way back
Through the old iron gate,
Standing open, painted black.

James Campbell is an author, lyricist, and poet residing in upstate South Carolina. He serves as the current Poet Laureate of West Pelzer, where he seeks to nurture a love of poetry, writing, and self-expression among those he has the privilege to walk alongside and to support community connections through the arts. jamescampbell@familyexcellence.net

Kira Carman

Autism

Of course it's not
your choice to remain
in your isolated internal world.
Such brilliant yet trapped intelligence,
and such a confusing onslaught
bombarding fragile senses.
What I would do
to know your world
from the inside out
and introduce you to mine,
but until I can
we will dance, learn, and grow,
"taught by an instinct
that so shall the silent abyss be
vocal with speech."*   *(R. W. Emerson)

Kira Carman writes spiritually themed poetry and prose. Her poetry has been produced on regional television when she lived in Pennsylvania. She has also written about her experience as an adoptee. As an EFT/Tapping Practitioner she enjoys supporting individuals with energy modalities. Kira currently lives in Myrtle Beach with her husband and impressive collection of beads.

Debbie De Louise

Leaving

The sun swallows my shadow
as I kick old dirt from the road.
The dust engulfs me in dreamlike fog.
I glance over my shoulder to see how far I've come,
but I can't see behind me. Even my footsteps are gone.
I turn, suitcase in hand, to the north,
but the future, too,
is clouded from my view.

I'm in a paradox of time
neither coming nor going.
I'm standing still.
Trapped in a maze
of my own construction.
Lost without directions,
I have nowhere to go.

Through the mist, I see a house,
one I've seen before, yet not the same.
an empty palace of stone.
Life no longer stirs within its walls and frame.

On the back porch, there's a hiding place beneath the eaves
where I concealed myself when I was four
playing hide and go seek

with some neighborhood boys.
and in a thunderstorm
when lightning was scarier indoors.
Now it frightens me more
to know I can't hide there anymore.

I enter the house
and walk from room to room.
Everything is familiar, yet strange.
I can feel the difference but can't locate the change.

I turn the doorknob to my bedroom
and find myself in a closet with a mirror.
But the reflection I see is a childhood me.
There's nothing to identify who I am today.
I close the door and walk away.

I go up to the attic
where the old toys are collecting dust --
the blonde doll my brother tore the hair out of;
the storybooks with yellowed, torn pages,
their dream world faded and destroyed
by adult concepts of reality;
the gold-leaf diary that was my birthday present when I was twelve.
Without its tiny key, it's locked forever.
I've lost the key to my life.

I walk out of the house
which disappears in the gloom
and follow the path
now lighted by the sun.

I've left that part of time
behind me in the darkness
after I was born
but years before I lived.
My suitcase is lighter in my hand,
my direction clearer.
I've learned that my destination becomes nearer
the farther I go.

Debbie De Louise, a retired reference librarian, writes two cozy mystery series. She's also written standalone novels and a book of cat poetry. as well as stories, and poems that appear in over a dozen anthologies. Debbie recently moved from Long Island to South Carolina where she lives with her husband, daughter, and two cats. Learn more about Debbie and her books by visiting her website at https://debbiedelouise.com

Mackenzie Doherty

The Fear of Forgetting

Sometimes pain is forgotten entirely...
The pain of missing you, is excruciating.
But the fear of not is even worse.
The fear of the unknown is terrifying but the thought of your voice
slipping from my mind is the scariest of all
I long for the memories I have forgotten though I can't help but fear
the thought of why they're gone from my head
I ask my brain what is there to protect me from
The pain I experience day after day?
The thoughts of what we could've done differently?
Fear of the future, the anxiety, the pain, the trauma
Or the love that shapes it all
The love that is rooted so deeply that I can't sleep thinking about you
I'm afraid to love again as if I do I could get hurt
What if they disappear
Just like you did
Fading day by day, memory after memory, like they were never there
to begin with
So I just won't
I won't love.
I will shut myself off from that part of my brain
Who needs it?

That works for a while. You hurt yourself and some others along the way, but it works.
You never have the chance to lose them.
Since you never loved them from the start

Mackenzie Doherty, a dedicated college student pursuing majors in Forensic Science and Chemistry. Alongside academics, Mackenzie finds solace and passion in music, expressing herself through guitar and vocals. Despite early adversity, Mackenzie has persevered, driven by a deep resilience that fuels her journey.

Matthew Eastland

Craggy Gardens

Here the road was blocked,
And with it some of my hope
For finding relief.
There was nowhere left to go
But back the way we came.
There had been no grand views,
No sights to reward the effort,
Just another failed idea.
Fog and clouds obscured.
But as I took the loop,
Ready to surrender,
There was a pathway.
I could feel the eyes on me
As I parked instead of driving.
What new insanity now?
I stepped out in my short sleeves
Into the rain and wind
On this cold mountain road
At the end of December.
The path was mud and logs,
Climbing into the trees
With no destination to see,
But it called out to me.
Now I was running,
Jumping, dodging across the path

To not fall in the icy puddles.
The cold and breeze embraced me
As I climbed higher.
There was the top of the hill:
Low stones ringed by trees,
Sky open but all hidden.
The wind swelled, while I stood
At the pinnacle,
As if to topple the trees and me.
It all should have been misery.
And yet,
I felt alive.
I felt alive!
The rushing sounds combined
To silence all the voices
Both within and without.
Had you been present,
You would have seen a drenched
And freezing fool within the storm,
But he was smiling
And would have stayed there
Had the real world not called him back.

Matthew Eastland is a native of Upstate South Carolina, where he lives with his wife and three daughters. This is his second time in South Carolina Bards. Through both his photography and poetry, he hopes to evoke feeling in others and has a joy for sharing ideas in different ways.

Caroline Eastman

Do Not Use Ladder

Do not use ladder near electrical wires.
Do not use ladder if it appears to be damaged or broken.
Do not stand on top rung or side of ladder.

Do not use ladder while dressed in a clown suit with
Painted face, baggy pants, and floppy shoes.

Do not gnaw on ladder, especially with false teeth.

Do not run with ladder

Do not allow dogs to use ladder
Except with proper supervision.

Do not use ladder as a bridge across the creek
Or to another dimension.

Do not use ladder for satanic rituals, lewd acts,
Or Tupperware parties.

Do not disassemble ladder to obtain parts for
Tables, tree houses or humanoid robots.

It would be best to leave the ladder
Securely placed in the storage shed
With the safety instructions laminated.

Be sure to carry it there with both hands.

Caroline Eastman moved to South Carolina to accept a position at the University of South Carolina in the Department of Computer Science and Engineering. Her research specialities included information retrieval, computer security, and computer science education. She is now retired and spends time birding, gardening, chasing trains, and volunteering for several organizations.

Bill Egan

Unity in Mourning

Peace, Comfort, Focus, even good memories
Some regret not making am mends -asking why?
or not making that last visit or phone call
- not saying goodbye

Each his own pain, but together we mourn
Let us mourn in unity- leaning together-
not falling down alone. A New hope is born
Love attaches each one as a fetter.

Arrangements, the phone calls to notify
The quiet moments of trembling broken
by our grievous strains. We cry cry cry cry.
Staring at each other- words unspoken.

Too soon, never ready. We needed more time,
but what of their body to cremate or bury with lime.

So many details to be worked out,
Not that we do this very often
Only a portion of THINGS prepared for,
 Oh no, forgot his old friend- he'll help carry the coffin.

Where will we put all of their stuff?
They kept this junk all these years!

It's tidy but, but I've had enough.
Then a mellow memory follows with tears.

In weeks other's sympathy,
even empathy will fade.
We appreciate caring-
sometimes aloof well wishes made.

And now each one stands alone
Individually say goodbye
We promise to gather before
another close soul should die.

Yes we have gathered each one
to grieve our own unique way
But opened to serve -to support
this Union at least for Today.

Bill Egan (aka +Bill [Cross Bill] on social media) has recently been exploring prose, poetry & verse. He's a professing Christian, husband & dad who derives inspiration from God's Word & creation. Bill has thrice been published in Statewide Anthologies including a piece in Haiku form. He's currently working towards joining his writings to musical composition.

Carley Eason Evans

The Absent Honeybee

While looking for a honeybee
Outside our kitchen window

In wildflowers standing tall
In the yard

A glimmering hummingbird appears instead
Along with butterflies

Young swallowtails clashing
Each other's colors

(One black and white
The other black and yellow)

And a gulf fritillary atop
A Mexican sunflower, boasting the same orange hue

Then one large Bumble bee striped with
Black and white and yellow alights
A bright red cone flower

While the honeybee is absent

Carley Eason Evans is an American novelist and poet who resides in the Low Country of South Carolina. Carley has been writing since the age of ten. She has written and published 17 novels, most recently IN A GRAIN OF SAND, THE WHOLE WORLD, available on Amazon in hardback, paperback, and e-book for Kindle.

Angela Feathers

For K

Her kisses are Merlot, dry
on my lips. My thirst
consumes me. She is bitter.
She is sweet.

She is intoxicating, but I'm
still standing.

Just a sip. Just a taste.
Just enough to make
the room spin.

I can stop whenever I want.
The giddy heat goes to my head.

I'm flushed and pink, and all
I see is her resolute mouth
approaching mine.

My heart leaps forward like a fish,
and I am burned at the stake.

Angela Feathers is a graduate of the College of Charleston's creative writing program with an emphasis in poetry. She spends most of her time wishing she was in her hammock and spending time with her two dogs. She writes because she knows no other way to be.

Jayne Jaudon Ferrer

Bound by Blood

Like Frost's poem, we two diverged
when our citrus-scented, small-town days
stopped short at the altar.
She of a serviceable skirt and
sensible pumps persuasion
left Main Street to see the world
on the arm of a naval commander.
I, the one with a penchant for accents,
intrigue, and adventures du jour,
stayed down South raising billy goats and boys,
one no less rowdy than the other.
Our paths cross from time to time.
More often, we engage in adagio duets
played with gusto in the key of fiber optics.
Her with news of the Smithsonian's latest exhibit,
the Ritz' recipe for lobster bisque—
me with tales of church bazaar projects,
belly flops in the backyard pool.
Lives shared in a series of vicarious tête-à-têtes,
trading triumphs, trivialities, and trials . . .
Who but sisters can explore—
in abject detail, infinitum—
original sin, suede after Easter,
the state of the union,
and skin tags?

Jayne Jaudon Ferrer is the author of seven books and the founder of www.YourDailyPoem.com. An award-winning copywriter and freelance journalist earlier in her writing career, Ferrer lives in Greenville, South Carolina. Learn more about her at www.jaynejaudonferrer.com.

Jennifer J. Foreman

Coming/Leaving Home

My stomach is now filled with its great carved stones
　/I have given up the river beds of my home
My legs have sunk into its mossy earth
　/I have left behind my blood ties in the marshy dirt with the cannon balls
It has crept into my bones, it's icy streams have found their way into my veins
　/The smell of salt of the ocean no longer flavors my breath
Its gray fog now flows down my chin
　/The summers brown tan has abandoned my skin
Its grass grows across my knees
　/I have waved goodbye to my sand swept feet
Its winds now wear down the peaks of my teeth
　/My mouth no longer waters for the taste summer peach
This is not the hill that I was born on
　/I was born just over the river
It is the one that I die on
And will be buried under

Jennifer J. Foreman is a born and bred South Carolinian, spending her most formative years in the Lowcountry. After graduating from College of Charleston with an English degree, she moved to Dublin Ireland to obtain her Masters degree in Creative Digital Media. And there she remains, having traded in her sandals for hiking boots, exchanged sunny mornings for foggy afternoons, and swapped cold sweet iced tea for hot cups instead (with lots of milk).

Renee Gahan

Postcard from the Hopis

I keep a postcard of Hopis in a broken frame.
At night they come out giggling and drift through my starlit house.
They look for glittering treats to hide behind their adobe rock.
Grandaddy can hardly keep from laughing and ruining the game.
In his frame he sits on a porch
and smiles
a Mona Lisa pout.

In sepia, the kachinas offer a peek at their trove.
A nest of thick twigs holding the sun like a pearl.
A sun bearer and tethered boy have hollows in their foreheads
where rousing
twilight sounds
and visions
dance the cosmic swap.

Granddaddy wears a tie and a fedora cocked on his forehead.
With a squeeze box at his feet, he holds up his banjo and guitar.
When I watch TV he's like a shy cat hoping to be seen.
His ghost peeks from the corner in baggy jeans and old man hat.
He never speaks.
I never see him clear as day,
only in dreams.

I wonder if they ever talk and dance on some dusky theme,
or while he plays the banjo, if the kachinas jig and shake,
or if they just meld and drift
like dust
in the afternoon light.
Don't take it seriously, you could go moon blind from gazing too much.
They don't, but then they do with both hands open,
inviting you to come and go
through your attic window frame.

Renee lives and teaches in Clemson. She has two kids, two cats and two dogs and three desks.

Jessica Gent

At Least

He's not actually abusive, they're just words after all.
How much harm can they do?

At least he doesn't hit me...

Actions speak louder than words, but words speak loud and clear.
It's hard not to believe the barrage of insults.

At least he doesn't hit me...

Words pierce and bore into my brain, taking root
in the mangled landscape until my thoughts are no longer my own.

At least he doesn't hit me...

I'm being sensitive and overdramatic.
Sticks and stones are what really hurt....right? I should be grateful.

I wish he would just hit me.

Jessica Gent has recently fallen in love with poetry after editing her employer's work. Her hobbies range from homesteading, traveling, cooking and now poetry. Her life goal is to have interesting stories to tell when she reaches her golden years.

Beverly George

Thing Made

The word "poem" translated from Greek means "thing made"
Keats called a poem "a form of escape."

Some say poems are words carefully chosen for their beauty
And sound arranged to share ideas, and emotions.

Blake said poetry was "to see a world in a grain of sand...
Hold infinity in the palm of your hand..."

We cannot "go gentle into that good night"
Thomas exhorts us "rage against the dying of the light".

Yet a poem can be seafoam, stardust, or a lighthouse on a rocky
Coast guiding us through birth, death and love.

A poem, this "thing made" like an oar moves waters
Of time until we reach its end
Asking for
More.

Beverly George is a retired public school music teacher who resides in South Carolina. She has two masters degrees in Education and earned National Board Certification in Elementary Choral Music. She self published a chapbook, *First Light* in 2022 which is available on Amazon. By the end of 2024 she expects to publish her second book of poetry. In 2025 she plans to have a family reunion with her two sons, daughter, three grandsons and sister in Sumter, S.C.

Meta m Griffin

My father's House

The steeple is slightly crooked.
Cold air moves throughout the sanctuary.
The foundation is uneven,
Somewhere a faucet drips. The pastor's
office door is open. A closed
bible is on a dusty desk.
Torn hymnals are scattered on the pews.
Light from the window shines on the alter.

Another threaded miracle
is created in a dark corner.
Restless spirits move through the trees.
they tell some other truth
that to love a body
Is more than a prayer,
a lonely, semantic chore.
off tune, off key
but gorgeous in its dissonance
like a hymn on Sunday.

An old man wanders down the halls.
A door slams. Roaring wind

creates a dissonance
like a twangy, off key Sunday morning song.
Not musical, but somehow gorgeous
in its imperfection.

Meta M Griffin is an activist, cat lover, and enjoys playing with words. Meta was an alternate for a SC Poetry Fellowship. She lives In Spartanburg, SC.

Sam Harrelson

You Gave It To Me

Your hand offered me the fruit,
a bitter and sweet testament
to our misunderstood desires.
Each bite deeper,
each chew a grinding realization
of the weight we now carry.
In your eyes,
the serpent's grin,
Truths we were never meant to know.
The world shifted,
colors more vivid, shadows stark,
the lamplight a beacon
in our newfound night.
I thought I heard the heavens,
but it was only the wind,
cold and indifferent,
sweeping through our undoing.
You and I, bound by the apple,
wander through the wilderness
of our own making,
seeking the elusive promise
of a return to grace.

Sam Harrelson is an educator and marketing strategy consultant in Spartanburg, SC. He has published works in religious studies, poetry, marketing, technology, artificial intelligence, and Assyrian art. He holds a Masters in Religion and Literature with an emphasis on ancient poetry and a degree from Wofford College in Religion.

Michael Hill

A Shapeless Thing

Every bone out of place
in space, in weightless anxiety
I break open, I'm flayed by the
heat, I'm a shapeless thing

My fluids curdle and spray
free, spreading to a thousand
worlds- a gift, a charity,
a million pieces of Earth let
out with belief- with an urge to
grow smaller, but travel further
into the long, quiet deep,
and they're all me-

They remember the Carolina spring...
They remember Clyde's, the breakfast
we had at three in the afternoon...
They remember who I was alone,
and who you were to me...

And so we're eternal-
a part of everything.

Michael Hill was born and raised in upstate South Carolina. He has a screenwriting degree from Western Carolina University and currently lives in Indian Land, South Carolina with his wife and son. He has published a number of poems and short stories in regional journals and also creates comics with his brother, artist R. Case Hill. Outside of writing, Michael is an avid film photography enthusiast and a full-time video editor.

Robert W. Hill

Flowers for the Flower Lady
--for Sara Moore, the Original

Black Lena, guarding the porch,
resists barking but clearly sees
the vulture standing in the grass

next to the mailbox over there
where the flower lady will come
to feed the colony of feral cats.

She will arrive in a white car
her late husband wanted because
he loved her and she works so hard

for us all—our florist, halfway
down Retreat Street—*Expressions
Unlimited* in a re-imagined house.

Though itself a sign, the vulture has
no name that we know of, but a few
more shuffle on the ridgepole, gable,

chimney of that house for sale for years.
Dour they loom, but today this one—
unnamed as far as we know—is alone

after the flurried flock cleared the dead
possum from the street a few days ago,
just as the flower lady had foreseen

—even before they showed their dark
red necks, their stark, featherless heads.
When I asked a friend to name the white

bush in the fenced yard, fronting that bird,
she wrote, "Hydrangea," but the lady
told me firmly, "No, it's Snowball."

As for the back-drop camellias, fire-falls
rouge the grass, die away about the base
and shall unfling the whole array. Sweet

Dresden! slaughterhouse of beauty, wreck
and rampage all undone, quiet in an instant.

Robert W. Hill taught at Clemson University, 1965-85, Furman and Erskine (summer sessions), before becoming English Department Chair at Kennesaw State in 1985. He and Richard J. Calhoun co-authored JAMES DICKEY (Twayne, 1982). Retiring in 2007, he now lives in Westminster with Jane, his wife of 43+ years, and two goldendoodles.

Jared Hove

22 April 2024

In our final days
Let there be only music

Words were plentiful and convenient
But insufficient

We built walls with words
They felt sturdy and durable

We paved paths with words
On occasion they led us to wonder

We dropped words into lakes
sometimes the ripples reached the shore

But deep down everyone knows
it was silence

then the first note of song
that made the difference

Jared Hove was raised in the United Arab Emirates and currently lives in Charleston, South Carolina with his family. He has lived and worked throughout the Asia, the Middle East, North America, and Europe. He loves poetry, reads it daily and, sometimes, writes a decent poem himself.

Laura Howard

His Love Lights Our Way

Light breaking through the darkness,
light that can never be put out,
for it has divine, HOLY power.
Sitting alone, feeling no hope is left,
Remember that JESUS is always near,
HIS LOVE will forever LIGHT our way.

Feeling to have no direction,
we now have HIS LIGHT,
a HOLY REFLECTION,
Guiding us with perfection.

LIGHT that soothes a grieving spirit,
who believes there is no limit.
JESUS' love shatters the doubt,
Providing LIGHT to all who feel.
all is now lost,
Lean on the Lord,
Let HIS LOVE now
LIGHT their way.

LIGHT that can heal, no matter the need,
just to the Lord, plead.
In trust and faith believe,
and ye shall receive.

JESUS IS THE LIGHT OF THE WORLD!
HIS LOVE LIGHTS OUR WAY!

LIGHT that seeps through our crippling fears,
LIGHT that wipes away our tears.
Taking time to pray,
HIS LOVE will forever
LIGHT THE WAY!!!!

HIS LOVE LIGHTS OUR WAY,
Oh, yes,
HIS LOVE LIGHTS OUR WAY!!!!

Laura is a highly regarded Christian poet known for her inspirational and motivational work that beautifully expresses the love of Christ. Her renowned piece, "When It Rains". was prominently featured in the SC Bards Anthology of 2023, and she has garnered further recognition with multiple poems published in other literary journals. With unwavering dedication, Laura continues to craft powerful poetry that speaks to readers. For more insights into Laura's profound poetry, explore more by visiting www.lulu.com/spotlight/christianpoetlaurafhoward https://lauraschristianpoetry.my.canva.site

Madi Huffman

You Shaped

As if my mind were being ratcheted open
Several new notches appeared
When I met you
Welcoming new revelations
New possibilities
Ones I didn't think were for me
You've turned this heart of stone
Back to fleshy throbbing beating
And breathed new life into
 you-shaped patterned breathing
Expanding horizons I had long closed
Exploding every door I juxtaposed
Mending my wings of tattered dreams
Sewing them back together with better seams
I'm chewing it over in the caverns of my mind
All the time
Still somewhat shocked & confused
On how I got this lucky
 ...Fortunate beyond reason
my life was blessed and renewed
The day I walked in and met you

Madi Huffman is a multifaceted artist based in various parts of South Carolina, originally hailing from North Carolina. She began writing poetry at a very young age encouraged by her mother who was also a poet. She is a southern girl to her core, always finding inspiration in her life experiences, the surroundings of growing up in the south, and the vast love of the human experience. She finds comfort in abstract concepts that describe every day events and hopes to create a visual experience when digesting her writings.

Debbie Hutchinson

Harvests

Tonight in English 553,
we discussed *Huckleberry Finn,*
and Twain's artistic use
of action verbs, his colorful cornucopia.

I did not make our bed this morning,
nor iron your shirts, so
your secretary will berate me
the first 15 minutes of your day.

I ate Chinese by myself and
dropped the fortune cookie
to the bottom of my purse
never reading the message
in its prophetic stomach.

How I dread the long drive home,
and the distance from you
that is further than miles
in this college classroom,
as my professor rattles on
of rivers, racism, and realism.

We will need to cut the okra tomorrow,
pull the corn, poison the weeds.
It will be October, a harvesting time
when we will reap some more
of what we have sown.

Debbie Hutchinson is a retired English and Creative Writing teacher, living on James Island...just miles from Folly Beach, South Carolina. Her poetry has appeared in many small press magazines, including THE HOLLINS CRITIC, THE DAVIDSON MISCELLANEY, THE LYRICIST, SOUTH CAROLINA BARDS POETRY SOCIETY 2023 and the late Tim McLaurin's novel, CURED BY FIRE, which received The Sir Walter Raleigh Award for best new fiction. The magic of words sustains her. She believes that words are the only comfort that does not leave our lives; everything and everyone else goes away.

Lucas James

Autumn's Head

bird skull found discarded by owl (who is feline of the air)
deceiving in its stillness,
watching a field mouse on the ground
diving on it like a bomb
the mouse reaching eternity.
meanwhile deer grow more desperate
displaced by downed trees,
deforestation in total darkness
they wait by the road,
headlights flash their lives before their eyes
before they are struck into oblivion,
murder, suicide, wild animals.
the summer's end leads creatures to madness
dying leaves, the sound of every step, the distant scent of
being burned in a pile.
cast a smoke offering into chilled air, while Jack-O-lanterns
guard doorsteps everywhere
their flames flinching in the darkness, casting silent spells.
soon enough their smiles will gnarl in grotesque rot
and be disposed with their candles burned out.
as waiting for winter draws to close meaning more madness,
darkness, sadness
colored lights, winter nights
celebrating life to survive.

Lucas James (26) has been writing poetry for seventeen years. He has produced over three hundred and fifty pieces (and counting) from poetry and short stories, to plays. He is actively seeking an audience for his work.

David Rhoades Johnson

Leaving At First Light

The boat is rigged and ready.
The gear has all been stored.
The tanks are filled to capacity,
And the Captain's now on board.

We depart today at Dawn,
Leaving at first light.
Grateful again for the memories,
As Manteo fades from sight.

But the wind is picking up
Bringing with it a new day,
And what that day will bring,
Who is there to say?

So cast off the bowlines,
And turn on the running lights.
Out beyond the breakers
Our future awaits, just out of sight.

David Rhoades Johnson is the award-winning author of six books of poetry, "Shadows of A Life", "The Sound of Falling Snow", "Navigating Uncharted Waters", "Tides of Shallowbag Bay", "Miles To Go", and "Pursuing The Far Horizon". He currently resides with his fiancé in the Village of Manteo on Roanoke Island.

Jerry T. Johnson

Remains

my world tossed by turbulence rattles
and shake. my ceilings cast hail, my
basements drop into hell and disaster
calls me on my cell phone greeting me
with an "Hello" and "this is nine one-one
calling you —and you are about to
have an emergency." My neighborhood
explodes into stabbings and shootings
and robberies and theft and graft and
lying politicians and creepy creeps
creeping into bedrooms, creepy creeps
creeping into boardrooms, creepy creeps
creeping into bank accounts and the assaults
and the assaults and the stealing and the
stealing and the rich remain the rich and
the help remain the help, and the slave remains
the slave and the poor remains the poor and
fools remain fools and idiots remain idiots
and liars remain liars and thieves remain thieves
and murderers remain murderers and the murdered
remain murdered and the slaughtered remain

slaughtered.

Jerry T Johnson is a Poet and Spoken Word Artist whose poetry has appeared in a variety of literary publications worldwide. Jerry is author of 2 poetry collections: "A Coldness" published by Finishing Line Press and "Poets Should Not Write About Politics" by Evening Street Press. His poetry collection "Poets Should Not Write About Politics" was selected winner of the Evening Street Press' 2020 Sinclair Poetry prize and his poem "The Apology" (Evening Street Press) was nominated for a Pushcart Prize in 2021

Debi Jones

Battle

They are kindred spirits, old souls perse.
It's a new drama every day.
Not paying for their mistakes, until the day they die.
Never losing their appetite.
Taking the wrong path, refusing to settle.
Dealing together with the battle.
They push the boundaries, but never cross them.
So caught up in their own problems.
Looking down a barrel of a life they couldn't control.
Watching their secrets unfold.
They were close to not existing, with no one to blame.
In the end, it all hurts just the same.

Kimberly June

Bookworm

Each wingbeat whoomps
FLIGHT
Skin and scale, claw and fang, muscle and sinew
A firebreather, the friend that carries us this day
Tomorrow a tardy rabbit
Last week a boy and a makeshift raft
Words on a page
A collection of letters, inked on paper
And then our walls dissolve to vapor
In their place a world anew
Senses awaken
Unbinding
Immersed
In those hours, the door is locked
All that weighs us floats away
Between the covers of our tome
We fight, we flee, we love, we laugh, we cry, we fall, we fly
A life we choose to step into
One chapter at a time

Kimberly June is a Charleston native and works in the tourism industry. She's an avid reader of all genres. A mother of three and a lover of the great outdoors, she considers writing to be free therapy.

Renee Kalagayan

Pharmacology

Keeping an appointment I was born to, I listened to my grandfather
As he prescribed that I must not become a poet. It is not proper.
My lot in life, he says, is to become a pharmacist. He is right.

I'm remembering his words in a waiting room as I count lines—
One, two, three, four—into bundles to be distributed.
I'm sending away the medicine to those whose bodies and minds
Are split, in the hope of making them whole again.

I take inventory of everything in this little box—the type, the size,
The shape—not one thing can be misplaced.
If I am wrong in any measure, it could cost a life.

With every written prescription I am taking souls into my hands,
Something I believed only God could do.
But in His leave, there are the pharmacists, counting away: one, two,
Three, four. There are the medications in high demand.

There are the poets.

Renee Kalagayan is a writer, MFA student, and publishing professional from Greenville. Her poetry has been published in *Inkwell Literary Magazine*, *Listening Journal*, and two other anthologies. She is a contributing editor for *Agape Review* and a poetry reader for *South 85*. She enjoys kaiju, horticulture, Gothic literature, and all things printed page.

Brittany Kay

Reign

A player on the neon stage for the world to behold
With Eckelberg's eyes fixed upon me
Bejeweled in adoration
Cloaked in glistening starlight
They say diamonds are forever

Icarus climbing on broken wings
Just one more time I must rise
Putting on a show for all
Wings clipped by the anchor dragging me down

But here in the upside down
I've got sick and twisted fascination
A darkness consuming me
My own decimation behind a smile

And when it all comes crashing down again
When the wolves are at the gate
I will light the match
And burn the way
After all, stars shine brightest in the darkness

From Simpsonville, SC, Brittany Kay is an international model and author, the reigning 2024 South Carolina Supermodel Icon, and former Ms. Palmetto Pride Plus America 2023. Her writing has been featured in various fiction and nonfiction anthologies. A graduate of Columbia College with a degree in Emergency Management, she has worked diligently to bring awareness to sexual assault and trauma recovery. In her free time, Brittany enjoys reading, motivational speaking, aviation, history, gaming, traveling, and spending time with her furbabies.

Rebecca Martin Kraus

Dad's Legacy

You filled up my childhood with story and song
You gave me the gift of your time
You taught me the love of words and of books,
And the intricacies of a rhyme.

You gave me your love of the pen and the page
Taught when to be wordy and when to be terse
How to create the right turn of a phrase
Whether serious prose or comedic verse.

You wrote for a living, made me want to write, too.
You were always composing for work or for play.
Your wordsmithing taught me the power within
To carefully craft the thoughts I convey.

Quiet by nature, no chatterbox you
An old typewriter your vehicle of choice
Your keen observations and kindness of heart
Always reflected in your writer's voice.

Words sung in music, folk and gospel,
Your melodious voice I loved to hear.
And the rhythm of the spoken word
Hiawatha and Shakespeare.

Thank you for your example, your legacy of words.
Through nature and nurture, you passed on your delight,
You gave me an infinite treasure
And I owe it to you that I love to write.

Rebecca Martin Kraus was raised in SC and received a degree in English & Sociology from USC-Aiken. Her journalist-father inspired her love of poetry in childhood and she has continued writing throughout her life. She and her husband reside in Murrells Inlet, SC.

Riley Legette

Spark

So often in life we lose sight of ourselves.
Whether we stamp it down to conform,
Or we have it beaten out of us,
By those who think it wrong.
We lose our spark,
The glimmer of our truest desires.
The starlight of freedom.
We forget how to be who we want,
Instead of who society thinks we should be.
But for some of us,
We keep hold of the spark,
We hold it deep inside ourselves,
Where not wind, nor rain,
Nor truly any force of man or nature,
Can take it from us.
And when the time is right,
That spark may be nurtured,
Into a roaring fire,
That will burn away all the incessant trappings,
Of a society that thinks it knows,
What's best and correct for all.
We will stand naked before the flame.

Born and raised in Charleston, Riley Legette is an up and coming poet. Grappling with often serious themes, she uses free verse to bring words to feelings. She writes in a powerful style that is easy to relate to and understand.

Faith Litchfield

conversations at the art gallery

there is a girl made of glass in the cleveland museum of art
she watches the people pass her by
they look at their reflections in her abdomen

"what a beautiful statue" they tell each other
"what a beautiful statue" they tell their reflection

there is something to say about reflections
(there is also something to say about glass)

there is a plaque made of bronze next to a girl made of glass in the
cleveland museum of art
the patrons could not tell you what it says
they ask the girl for her name
to only hear an echo of their question

"what is your name" the patron says
"what is your name" the plaque responds

there is something to say about echoes
(there is also something to say about emptiness)

there is a bench made of stone across from the plaque made of bronze
next to a girl made of glass in the cleveland museum of art
people sit but they do not look at the girl
they rest their feet and return to better pieces of art

"are you ready to go?" says the man
"are you ready to go?" says his wife

there is something to say about rest
(there also is something to say about neglect)

there is a girl made of girl on the bench made of stone across from
the plaque made of bronze next to a girl made of glass in the cleveland
museum of art
she says nothing
so nothing echoes

"hello" says the girl
"hello" says the glass

there is something to say about girls
(there is also something to say about glass)

Faith Litchfield grew up in Cleveland, Ohio but developed a love of writing when she moved to Sumter, South Carolina. She is passionate about the arts and has a deep appreciation for poetry and philosophy.

Kathryn Etters Lovatt

Cleaning Out

I wake to early trains,
rise and walk into a morning
where my birds wait
for their feeders to be filled.

The fattened doves understand
I am neither cat nor hawk. A pair
balance side-by-side on the curve
of a shepherd's hook, coo and stare.

They consider me with what feels
like kindness, and if there's
something kinder than the eyes
of a dove, I can't name it.

By afternoon, everything in me
aches. Relief comes in water
steamy enough for ghosts to rise
from Epsom and lavender.

They follow outside, sit with me
and listen to the remains of a hickory.
This one stood her ground for
six, seven human lifetimes.

What a fire she will set this night,
hot enough to eat my words:
the burden of journals, half done
poems & stories,

letters of men I loved,
and of women. Whether
I made music or whether
I only made noise,

my pages will lift and curl,
turn from flame, to spark,
turn into a hiss of false starts,
confessions, slips of smoke.

Kathryn Etters Lovatt lives and writes in Camden SC.. Her chapbook, Where Comparison Ends, and her collection of short stories, How to Euthanize a Fish, were published by Main Street Rag.

Angela Mason Lowe

Many Hands

There are hands dearly missed
Aged hands once young
that loved and cared for you

Generous hands that give
and hands that take
Strong hands that play us tunes

There are hands that help
…hands that heal
Sly hands that hide the truth

Hands that point
the way to go
and those that see us through

Calloused hands
with gentle touch
Hands that speak words, too

Sad angry hands
fist clenched tight
…only loving hands can soothe

Beware of idle hands
Find something good
that they can do

Appreciate the hands that pray
Those are the hands
to hold on to

Angela Mason Lowe's writing journey began with poetry. She soon established a visual-sharing group, Pegasus Poets II and presently serves as president of the Foothills Writers Guild of Anderson, South Carolina. *Full of Grace and Grit* is her memoir in poetry form. Her greatest accomplishment are the two volumes of *Vets Helping Vets Anderson: In Their Own Words*, stories of those who served in the military. Lowe is presently working on the third volume.

Neil MacAulay

Never Forget You

Some days, I fear I'll forget you, something so precious, so dear. Your voice, your smile, your tears - they're etched in my memory. Our dreams are what make us human, our hearts what make them real. You dream of me, I'll dream of you, and together we'll reach the heavenly stars. The stars shine bright, guiding us through the darkness. The night awaits, will you walk with me through its shadows?

Neil MacAulay was born in Charleston, SC. Coming from a large family he is number 9 of 10 children,

Natalie Malone

Purple
Imitation of Prado's Poem Purple

Lavender a shade of purple is the color of my aura
which a friend told me months ago.
Purple is his soul but he bleeds red.
Purple are flowers that grow wild in
the Georgia fields.
Purple is the color of my favorite vine. Wisteria.
Purple is the hair that curls on my grandmother's
Roommate's head.
Their minds wander in and out of the 1960's.
Purple are the bruises that I have on my body from
running into tables, chairs, and bumping into corners of doorways.
Purple is my favorite color!
Purple the color of the poetry that I write.
Purple is the sunset in Georgia.

My darkness is purple.
I like to hide in my darkness.
It's where I belong.
My purple security blanket is the darkness.
Heaven's light is purple.
The purple light looks inviting and I walk in the purple light.

Natalie Malone graduated from College of Charleston with a Creative Writing Degree with the emphasis in Poetry. Natalie spends her days with a cat in her lap and a 6 year old telling her about his day. Natalie still continues to write and hopes to have a collection of poetry published in the future.

Robert Matheson

Time to Rest

Consumed in soft petal drapery
Yellow sugar shines
How does it feel when your wings get tired?
Does it happen this time of year?
Under a pink flower moon
As your knees flex
You fall over, sideways
Lay your head on my chest
While wrapping your legs around mine
Buzzing

Robert Matheson is a community engaged artist living and working in Newberry, South Carolina. His work focuses on improving the well-being of others through the arts. In 2021, Robert installed his first "Poetree", a safe community space where creatives can express themselves through writing. Poetree examples can be viewed here: https://www.robertmatheson.com/poetrees

Elaine Mathis

Bella's Return

She glides in darkness towards the shore,
encased in russet armor with yellow shield,
her majestic beauty recognized by few.

Survival—her focus since piercing soft shell.
Benign, yet with many antagonists
threatening her kind.

Blossomed, she returns to her genesis;
driven by instinct that refuses denial,
following the map imprinted on her memory.

Her oversized head emerges, surveys. All is safe for now.
She drags her vulnerable mass across the cool sand
to fulfill her destiny.

Soon night will give way to day.
Crowds will gather to witness the brilliant sun
cast dancing diamonds across the rippling pewter.

She must hurry! Exposure is an enemy.
Her hind flippers carve a life hole nestled by dunes;
here, she lays and tenderly covers her creation

then, indulges in a brief pause...

Designed as creator, not protector—she must leave.
Guided by friendly moonlight, she inches away and
delves back into the night Atlantic.

A native South Carolinian, Elaine G. Mathis earned a B.A. in Journalism and has always enjoyed writing. Her work has been published by Hallmark and CaringBridge. Elaine is also an avid wildlife photographer. She lives with her family in Columbia. *In honor of our state reptile, the loggerhead sea turtle*

Elmore McLeod

Cigarette Light

i never thought i could hate
i'm not even sure what hate is anymore

because i hate you
at least i should
and yet i miss you
i shouldn't; i didn't think i could

i miss the potential of you
i miss what you were supposed to be
i miss who you used to be

i wish i could go back to the days when you were kind
when you would braid my hair in early mornings before school
when you would make the chicken noodle soup i loved so much
more than anything i wish i could go back to the days when i was
small and you would sing to me
i wish i could hug my mother one more time

but the mother i loved is gone
i don't know when she left, but she's been gone for a long time
the husk of what remains is not the woman who was supposed to
protect me
what remains is something wicked

you robbed me of so much
but she would never hurt me
she didn't have the power to hurt me
the mother i mourn would rather stick a needle in her eye then ever see me cry

but you are not her

when i look at you i don't see her
i can't; i won't
i only see your face in the night, lit by cigarette light
the darkness in your eyes gives me chills
the coldness in your words haunts me

i can't even picture her smile anymore
and it's horrifying

whenever i see the face my mother used to wear i feel nothing but fear
fear for the nights you screamed
fear for the sound of footsteps
fear for my sisters, who you robbed just the same
fear that I'll always be broken
most of all i fear too much of you lives in me; i fear that one day i'll look in the mirror and see your face staring back

i fear that one day you would come back

i fear that i'd let you in

im paralyzed with the fear that you could hurt me again

that you would hurt me again
because you will always find more to take
you always seek to fill your own cup, but you never take notice the hole in its bottom
you take and take and take, you continue to take until every else's cups have run dry
but you never give back

maybe because you don't have anything left to give
because you are broken
maybe because you are as broken as I am

because someone broke you first

i only hope that one day you learn how to mend yourself
but the day that you do, i will not be there
i will never be there
because i can no longer picture her smile
i only see your face in the night, lit by cigarette light
and that has haunted me for far too long

Elmore McLeod is a queer aspiring writer from Sumter, South Carolina. Their biggest inspiration is their sister Samantha and they love the color purple an oddly unhealthy amount.

Samantha McLeod

Abandoned

My mother is gone and yet
She surrounds me.
She is my coffee cup with stars and moons
-she is the guilt that surfaces for shoving the mug to the back of my cupboard, ignored.
She is the grilled pineapple at the Brazilian Steakhouse
-she is my hesitance to admit how much I love it, to admit how similar I might be to her.
She is the haybale for the horses
-she is the poisonous curiosity about her new home in Oklahoma.
She is the growl in my throat when I lose my temper with my children.
She is the flood of tears pooling in my eyes when the world becomes too much.
She is the disgust at my own reflection
The inner monologue pounding through my skull, one word over and over
Burden. Burden. Burden.
She is the woman who bought me an ice cream sandwich when I got my first period.
She is gone.
And I have to remind myself everyday that that is exactly where she wanted to be.

Samantha McLeod is a writer, a seeker, and a wanderer. She is a mother and a wife. Most importantly, she is a human doing life and finding herself a little more everyday.

Catelyn Cecile Meeker

The Secret Lives of Birds

The bird himself has no care, save for the worm wriggling in the soil beneath his feet.
The pretty robin's red breast protrudes and he delicately hops, listens to the ground, scoops up the worm in his beak, & again takes flight.
Soon the cardinal, (this one with dull-colored feathers, for she is female) comes to sit atop the fence & sing to me. Her vibrantly red-feathered partner always joins, & when they fly away their wings move so violent a gust of wind that I hear each extending feather flutter past.
We could learn from these birds; we too could sing of the vigor that living a full life brings.
I hear their morning and evening songs, rapid and fierce with infectious joy.
Why can we not possess such joy?
Pretty robin,
Melodious cardinals,
Your chirping brings me to tears.

Catelyn Cecile Meeker is 34 years old and lives in Myrtle Beach, South Carolina. She moved to Myrtle beach two years ago from a small town called Moundsville in West Virginia. Along with writing poetry, she also loves to write short stories, to paint, to sing, and to be consumed by a good book! Her wish is to expose both the beauty and the devastation of the human experience that is life in her poetry. She has been writing both poetry and short stories since childhood. Thank you for your consideration of her poetry in this South Carolina anthology.

Stacey Militana

A Glance at Sunset

She stops
Only a moment
Stealing a glance at her lover

Tall and handsome still
Though jet colored hair is now streaked with silver
And years of laughter have mapped their way
Across his face

He looks back at her
As they stand in the sunset
A feeling of warmth, of home sets in
As he holds her hand in his

Just a moment
A single glance
So full of love
Full of memories and time deeply cherished

Stacey originally hails from Upstate New York. She is an avid reader of whatever she can get her hands on. Her biggest dreams are to write professionally like her hero, Margaret Atwood, and to travel the world. She enjoys observing people and making notes on what she sees.

Connie L. Montgomery

Lighthouses

A beacon in the night,
A North Star for guidance and an
answer to prayers in the storms of life.

Seas roar and the wind blows but the light is on in the top of the dwelling; beckoning and calling the weary traveler. Come and be rescued and find rest. Run and never give up you are safe.

The lighthouses are the roadmaps for a journey that ends well.

Connie L. Montgomery is a retired occupational therapist. Currently she is the author of a Children's book "Letta Forgives" the first in a series, a healthcare reference booklet entitled "You're Not Just A Number- Putting CARE back into Healthcare" and a coming of age teen novel titled "Nellie Knows Best". She has been married for 33 years to her husband, Dwayne Graham. They have two, young adult children.

Susan Mouw

Christmas Morn

Christmas morn dawns bright and cold
With snow thick upon the ground.
Children squeal with glee, their wishes fulfilled
And joy and laughter abound.

The tree, once bright, now sags with the weight
Of the lights, and the many shiny balls.
Its day, once anticipated, has now come and is going.
The needles, now dry, silently fall.

The stockings, once hung o'er the mantle with care,
Are now emptied of their secret stash.
The candy cane wrappers and empty battery packages
Now litter the floor with the rest of the trash.

Forgotten are the recent memories
Of the shopping, the rush, and the noise.
Soon forgotten, too, are the mountains of gifts –
The ties, the socks, and new toys.

Is this what You meant for Christmas, Lord?
Are we honoring the memory of Your Birth?
When the TV stations track Santa's progress
From the North Pole to the ends of the earth.

But so few words are spoken
In memory of what this day truly means.
So few thoughts turn to You, Lord
In the rush of this holiday scene.

I truly love this season, Lord.
I like the lights, the gifts, and the noise.
I like Christmas carols sung by the fire
And children's faces as they open their toys.

But, even more, I love the memory we honor.
The joy and miracle of Your Birth
That promises of our salvation
And hints at Your sacrifice, and its worth.

So, this Christmas day, amid the rustle of paper,
And shouts of joy and acquisition
I promise to remember You, Lord
And what it means to be a Christian.

Susan Mouw was raised the middle child in a military family. Her career spanned 20 years in application development, mostly within the financial community and included a short stint in the US Army as an electronic signals intelligence analyst. She is now retired and lives with her husband in mid-state South Carolina.

Emily O'Neil

Magnolia Yearning

I stood still on the edge of the concrete path in the serene garden.
I was walking towards a magnolia tree.
I was looking at the beautiful flowers growing inside.
Suddenly, a mighty wind begins to blow hard.
I quickly moved far away from the tree hiding near a rose bush.
The leaves and flowers are shaking violently.
They remained diligent with determination not to fall to the ground.
Yet, their defiance is in vain.
 The leaves and the magnolia tree start to fall slowly creeping with the wind.
Remarkably, one stem from the magnolia tree continues to hold on for dear life.
The stem is wrestling with the strongest wind maintaining its brutal force.
I stood back wondering at the thought of a single stem from a magnolia tree battling against this great wind.
The magnolia stem seems to be yearning for its existence.
In the end, the stem is steadfast in its effort to survive tall preserving itself during the raging wind.
So, my people, be like the stem growing from the magnificent magnolia tree,
Continue to fight for your existence in spite of life's circumstances.

Emily O'Neil has always loved the power of words spoken and written since childhood. She believes that words carry meaning to inspire, motivate and encourage herself and others with her writing. Emily currently living in Bennettsville, South Carolina, is the author of the poetry book Hope in Victory Encouraging Lessons from Forgiveness and Acceptance Within and the creator of the inspirational blog Everyday Operations to Inspirational Living. Professionally, Emily has attained degrees in English and Business Leadership as well as has worked several years in retail management.

Gene Owens

The Heavenly Body

No artisan of earthly fame
Could sculpt the contours of your frame,
Nor earthly genes your form devise;
The great computer in the skies
Components gleaned from worlds afar
And programmed you for what you are.

Some star in agony of death
Breathed with a searing cosmic breath
That, beaming 'cross ethereal skies,
Bequeathed the sparkle in your eyes.

The gold that lights your lustrous hair
Came from some lesser luminaire
That spun a web of golden hue,
Someday to make a crown for you.

From out the Milky Way there flowed
A formula to each anode
That, streaming through the glossy night
Ordained your skin galactic white.

Each line of your exquisite shape
Was programmed on magnetic tape,
And from these electronic tomes

Were charged the pregnant chromosomes
That made of you a perfect gem,
Beyond the art of IBM!

Retired journalist Gene Owens has been senior associate editor of The Virginian-Pilot in Norfolk, Va., editorial-page editor of the Roanoke Times & World-News in Roanoke, Va., and assistant managing editor and metro columnist for the Mobile, Ala., Press-Register. He is a native of Clinton, S.C., grew up in Aiken County. and now lives in Anderson.

Tony Owens

Port Royal

Breathing water, you walk beneath live oaks,
Moss hangs like beaded curtains in the
door

Of *Sister Soul*, fortune teller and palm reader,
Who will pierce the fog of the future for a fee.

Moss swings in the warm wind off the sound
And sways like clothes drying on a line.
The line is filled with underwear and sheets,
White sails languid in the liquid light.

The small gator has overstayed the tide,
His tail oscillates like a fish as he slides
Away. He leaves a trail in the bright mud
And disappears into the marsh.

In an old photo, your mother stands
On a windy beach, her long cotton dress
Blown like white caps on the gray sea,
She has turned to wait for you,

One arm reaches back for you
In permanent beseeching.

Tony Owens is a retired educator and consultant who currently teaches classes on philosophy and music at OLLI/Furman in Greenville. His first book of poetry, *Keowee River Songs*, was published in 2022 by Redhawk Press of Hickory, NC.

Tolar Parker

Ebony Blades

I was a raven
Dark, noisy, and quarrelsome
Not answering to anyone's call but my own
Remaining a transient scavenger, feeding on my own cursedness
A day came when new winds carried my marred wings to distant lands
It was there I saw her
A cardinal so lovely and highlighted with warm elegance
Singing her cantata for the one who would listen
And how I listened
How I longed
To disrobe from my own ebony blades and vanquish my black beak's shrilling symphonies
With each note from her brightly colored bill, a vibrancy broke through the midnight plumage
Molting before me until I was cloaked with carmine
I slowly sang a soft sonata for her and received her response in kind
Echoing through a hushed forest
Our song
Our song
Of waiting
Of yearning
Of searching
Of finding
Finally finding

Tolar Parker. He's like a Ramones concert. He's loud. He's fast. And your parents probably won't like him.

Jessica Rainey

Absolution

A cut so deep
That even I can't weep
Blood rushing
Tears gushing
The words you said
Made you dead
I run into the dark
Like a disgraced monarch
Plotting for revenge
This won't be the challenge
You fought with words
I retort with blood soaked swords
Darkness will rise
I will be your demise
Knowing I once loved you
Remembering I said 'I Do'
Next time I see your eyes
You will want to apologize
My pain became too much
But it won't be enough
I cannot stand you any more
I need to be alone, heal my core
I will come for retribution
I am your absolution

Jessica Rainey is a full time masters student while being a full time stay at home mom. She is dedicated to helping her children and others learn while simultaneously enjoying the life of being the wife and mom of a military family.

Arthurine Rice

Beach Lovers' Elation

It was a warm soft, starry and moonlight kind of night. A man and woman dazzled and mesmerized by their love. They had no desire to see the coming of a new morning sunlight. They strolled with hands entwined on wet warm beach land. Their feelings were of elation anticipating sharing warm kisses. She is his lady of preference, he is her mighty king of a man! They loved without concern about strangers passing by. Like Ocean and land embracing without shame, so did they. He is the owner of the beautiful beach is the reason why. He is in love and thinking about giving her his last name! Tantalizing sea breezes engulfed them, coercing and igniting sweet sensations as he lifted her for another tongue exchange . He whispered in her ear, I am yours, you will always be mine! And then, another lip/ tongue dance exchange occurred as she wondered if his warm seducing kisses would thrill her every time! Forced by a potent gravitational pull they again tenderly kissed lips. She alone could instantly enflame burning sensations within him with her walk and those eye catching movements of her erotic full hips! With swiftness he lifted her from her feet and anxiously carried her to their room filled with sweet Rose petals. He proposed! Prior to morning sunlight they were married!

Arthurine is a published Poet who has shared her work on sites such as Facebook, Instagram and various groups on the Internet. Arthurine is a retired State Government Social Worker.

LaToya Richburg

My Flower

One day as I was walking along the roadside
I glanced over my shoulder and a flower caught my eye
It was not special in color, the petals were not rare
This flower was not abundantly blooming, it was just there
Alone in a field, no other flowers around
It peeked through the grass, just barely above ground
As I paused from walking to give this flower a gaze
Thoughts flooded my mind so, until I was in a daze
I could uproot this flower and bring it to my home
Why should something so beautiful be out here alone
I can keep it in a pot on a windowsill in the sunlight
I will talk to it, use it for inspiration when I write
This flower would have such great care if I bring it home with me
Yet still I had to ask, is my home where the flower should be?
This flower may be alone now, but what if it's just beginning to grow
What if this flower is a start to a garden that nature has begun to sow
It is the spark of beauty standing in the midst of a common field
This flower so unconditionally shares its beauty with passersby willing to yield
Just like me, I stopped to see as I was walking along the roadside
So for now I will visit and allow it to bloom in the beauty of its time

LaToya Richburg is a native of South Carolina. She is the author of a published poetry book entitled *Ministering Thoughts* available on Amazon, Barnes & Nobles, and Yorkshire Publishing. LaToya is currently working on other books she hopes to have published soon. The support of her wonderful husband and two beautiful children are an inspiration.

Jim R. Rogers

Pre Mature__

His son was barely born he said,
a few ounces only came from her,
so small, hard to tell exactly what he was
holding on to the edge of life with
fingers not yet formed enough to
clutch so others grabbed on for him,
made a promise he would not die, to
leave them almost cheering.
love, grit and pure resolve along
with medical wonders put him in
warming ovens adorned with
tubes and pipes that kept the life
pouring in and through the hair like
veins pumping, giving juice to make
him grow for five months there.
He became the boy, the child they
ordered, even with built in delays,
they took him home to start the
trip that would take him where
he surely came to go.

89 going on 90, poet and parenting educator Jim R. Rogers keeps on with his efforts to be a decent writer. He has a Master's degree in early childhood education, has authored a book on effective parenting, and has four grandsons and one great grandson. He adores his wife and his dog and lives in Surfside Beach, SC. He is happy.

Ron Roth

The Bicyclist

As I fumbled with an air pump
an old man, gaunt and lean
like John Lee Hooker
ambled over to me
from his bicycle laying
on the parking lot curb.
I've seen these men on their bicycles
hugging the edge of the road,
threading the white paint strip
like daredevils.

"Can you spare a quarter sir?"
I snap back, "Not now pal, not now."
Pouring down, the rain
soaked me as I searched
for a fugitive tire-valve cap.
Walking back to his bike,
his shoulders drooped
under a neon, orange vest.

I collapse into the car,
slam the door and rev the engine.
My wife says gently,
"Aren't you going to give him something?"
I look over the steering wheel

into the gray rain thinking,
what was it some philosopher said?
"Never resist a generous impulse."
Got out of the car
and pulled out a five,
handed it to the man.

He smiled gaily,
stunned by his good luck.
Danced back to his bike,
leaping like one of the Nicholas brothers
snapping his taps.

Ron Roth's fiction and poetry have been published in literary magazines throughout the United States. His 2019 poetry collection, *Awake To Every Grace,* was described by Susan Meyers, winner of the South Carolina Poetry Prize, as a "celebration of the human spirit as well as the myriad beauties of the world." His recent collection of poetry, *This Peculiarly Peaceful Light,* was published in 2023 by Kelsay Books.

August Sage

Spring

I think - sometimes
And often too much
But I think that I am reaching for something
That I am no longer able to find

A version of myself that doesn't exist anymore
The files have been deleted
Wiped from the hard drive
I can't go back to who I was before -

Because who I was before wasn't real

I try to turn to the beginning of the book
But the pages are all blank
Scattered phrases stretched thin
Across twenty seven years of confusion and delusion

Pretending and defending
Exchanging one mask for another - like some sort of twisted masquerade.
Even now - I reach for a mask
But they've all crumbled to dust

The carnival's been left to rust
Underneath the new rain of Spring.
And I'm not sure what flowers will bloom in its place.
What vines will crawl over the broken equipment

What trees will burst forth through old coping mechanisms
What new me will be born from this new beginning.
Because I can't go back -
But I don't know how to move forward.

The rain continues to pour -

The ground saturated
Waiting for the sun to emerge from behind stormy clouds
For the seeds to sprout
For things to begin.

And yet -

Here I sit.

August Sage is an upcoming poet, having moved to Charleston fairly recently. They have been writing poetry for as long as they can remember, using their free form style as a way to explore deeper, often darker, themes. They find inspiration in imagery, using vivid descriptions frequently in their work. This is their first time publishing any of their work.

Joanna Schuman

These Lines are for You

These lines are for you. Take them,
both offering and confession.
I ask not forgiveness nor beg for absolution,
quite simply, all I seek from you is love.
Once I believed only romance novels
bespoke an irrational love like mine.
You, a priest, vowed to celibacy,
I, married, with devoted husband and children.
Unknowingly, you have taught me
a dozen different ways to spell desire.
I find myself incandescent with love.
You have lighted new fires
at abandoned altars in my heart.
Loving you, I have been transfigured.
My mirror reflects a mysterious stranger,
eyes dark with longing, lips parted,
waiting to be kissed.

These lines are for you. Take them.

Quickly read them. Time grows short.

Already the ink is beginning to burn my fingers.

At any instant the paper itself may ignite.

Joanna Schuman has been writing poetry since the age of seven. She is a member of the Olli Writer's Workshop in Clemson, SC. She enjoys writing, reading, cooking, delights in the changing seasons of upstate South Carolina and spending time with her large family and longtime friends.

Patricia Shea

Aggressor's Ride

September eleventh two-thousand and one
All things as usual the day had just begun
Stock market trading ...winners and losers invading
Typical business of the day...stock market traders at play...

While ill-fated citizens in yet another place ...
The beauty of a new day....
 They thought they were going to embrace...
How ironic it was.... that they
Unknowingly they sealed their fate...
By boarding their flights on that fateful date...

Seven- Sixty- sevens slowly making their way
For those on board their lives the last day
Scrambling to make amends
Words that they thought but never quite said
"Dad I love you ...we are going to die..."
"I had to get in touch with you...
I just had to say "goodbye"....
I'm sorry there's nothing we can do...
In a few fatal moments you'll know this to be true...
Our country is being invaded...
Our innocence is gone ...
At the hands of the aggressors ....
We were simply just the pawns...

Eight- Forty-eight in the morning ...
Without any previous warning...
Tower one was taken out...
While People in the streets ....
Looked on in unbelieving doubt...
"This can't be happening!" ...
"Please say it's not true...."
Not but a few moments later ...
A second plane took tower two....

Can't anyone stop this fate ...
Why do these people use us
What is it that propels their hate ...
The impact of it was astounding...
Fallings debris and thunderous pounding ....
People in the streets in smoke they were drowning...but ...
The passengers were silent their terror was finally gone.

Eight- forty- eight in the morning
Their day was forever done...
The aggressors that had fueled their terror
Had momentarily won ...

What was once a nation divided?
Petty differences now subsided...
We are again together united...
All of us humbled as we were ...
Once again reminded...
That terror was making its way.... to us

Not to take freedom for granted....
To wave our flag proudly...
Lives were lost to cover the cost...of freedom...

Written in honor of those that lost their lives on September 11th, 2001. May we never forget them

---

A retired Senior Quality Engineer from Canton Ohio, Patricia Shea currently resides in Greenville South Carolina. She enjoys writing poetry that describes various life events. Enclosed are two poems that were written by her. She has over 40 poems to choose from.

Peggy Shrum

Daydream

I rose, again, today
to become the sun.
To lift my light, tired,
so heavily laid
upon the horizon,
and climb alone
into the sky.

I drew down, from there,
the angel-shaped shadows
of hawks over fields,
shadows which clung
to the grasses,
danced,
then vanished.

I coaxed open
the clenched petals
of tight-fisted flowers
tendered shy
on restless vines,
and called upon leaves
to lean in
and face me.

I saw myself shine,
lit up and vivid,
in eyes,
squinting skyward,
as they offered
to show me
a more worthy blue.

I seeped myself
through treetops, down,
searching for ground,
and there, laid my remains
in torn, tattered patterns,
scattered and stretching
across the forest floor.

I lingered, diminishing,
later, and lower,
the last of my tasks
to sketch the trees
in lengthening,
pencil-line strokes,
upon the binding horizon,
and I wondered, then,
if tomorrow's blue
would hold me.

Peggy Shrum is a Wildlife Biologist residing in the foothills of upstate South Carolina. Ms. Shrum is an avid explorer and wilderness enthusiast with a particular passion for birdlife. Her reverence for the natural world inspires her as a poet and creative essayist.

Amanda Britton Smith

Radio Silence

When I was forty-five, I began to sense that
Radio silence was preferable to Friday night fights.
Preferable–but, oh, so boring. Few things match the rush of
An uppercut to the spleen or a body hook to the ribs.
Who wants to sit and think of pithy things to say,
And then use all of the self control available not to say them?
I write them down for myself, laugh out loud at my wit,
And punch the wall.

Amanda Britton Smith is a native of Hemingway, South Carolina, and she is a graduate of Francis Marion University. Mrs. Smith has lived in several locales across the Southeast, and she currently resides in Virginia with her husband and children, where she teaches high school English.

Angela Thomas Smith

Whispers of the Coastal Breeze: South Carolina's Beach Bliss

Sun-kissed waves upon the shore,
Whispers of the ocean's lore.
Golden sands that stretch so far,
Underneath the twinkling stars.
Seagulls dancing in the sky,
Rhythmic waves, a lullaby.
Salt-kissed breeze, a gentle touch,
Nature's beauty, oh so much.
Palmetto trees swaying tall,
Echoes of nature's call.
Laughter and joy, in every sound,
South Carolina's coast, so profound.
With every sunset, every tide,
The beauty of this place abides.
A sanctuary for the soul,
Where waves of tranquility roll.

Angela Thomas Smith, a prolific author, esteemed coach, and visionary owner of a renowned magazine and podcast, is hailed as the Queen of Collaborations within the literary and empowerment spheres. Known for her ability to bring together diverse voices and perspectives, Angela has built a reputation for fostering creativity, connection, and positive change through her collaborative endeavors dedicated to uplifting others, Angela embodies the motto: "I am the change I desire to see in this world."

Jeff Snyder

Troubled Heart (Revival)

You do the work God gives you then depart.
As the crow lauds a new day I grow old.
Our songs and stories fade to twilight, cold
aged embers belie a sanguine start.
The spirit wrestles angels in the dust
of dreams and forgets in the waking morn
the struggle. New found vigor now adorned
with virtue aids, avoids a breach of trust.
In dawning light a witness can in error,
misinterpret evidence left behind,
a reminder for you to bear in mind
or offered to almighty God in prayer.

See how creation pauses then imparts
revival so now calm your troubled heart.

Wendy Soltis

He smoked a cigarette
On Yom Kippur, which means
He lit a fire and I asked
Why. He said the rule on fire
Was only for the holiest of days,
The Sabbath, Shabbos, Shabbat,
(interpretations, translation,
transliteration) And on the 7th day thou shall rest
From all endeavors. But I asked
On that 7th day, and he explained.
No rest for the weary rabbi on this
Day of no fire. Only this day, he explained
To me. But what of god, I asked,
That vengeful God we learned about?
But what about water in the desert
He countered. But what about
Moses, who was impatient,
Gave up a life of luxury and didn't
Get to enter the Promised Land, and
What about Joshua who killed every
Man-woman-child so he could?
Come back here, old man, my rabbi,
My teacher. Come back here
And explain all this to me so
I can stop these tears that fall
Because I can't believe Jesus
Meant for all the little children to suffer
And go to him only after death.

Wendy is a retired teacher/trainer who has been writing poetry since her teens. Most of her poetry is her attempt to understand life and all its puzzlements. She is a misplaced Jersey Girl residing in South Carolina, where it became possible for her to have a horse in her life (one does not own a horse anymore than one owns a friend.)"

Tyler Spencer

OCD

I wash my hands obsessively after I touch a doorknob,
But when you kiss me—
I lick your spit off my lips
Like it's the last drop of water
In the middle of a scorching hot desert.

I crave you
Like a bird craves sky.
I want you
Like a frog wants to hop.
I need you
Like my head needs a pillow.
I love you
Like it's the very last time.

Tyler Spencer, better known by his stage name "Melodramatic", is a South Carolina artist, musician, singer-songwriter, 35mm film photographer, & published poet. This DIY approach is a sentiment he applies to his poetry as well. Drawing from an eclectic array of influences like Charles Bukowski and Sylvia Plath, his chaotic, avant-garde artistic style reflects his penchant for finding love and meaning in the seemingly mundane. Melodramatic recently released his latest EP, "Flies of Hunger", a captivating sonic journey that combines the styles of indie and post-country, akin to artists like Elliott Smith, Alex G, and Radiohead. Available on Spotify, Bandcamp, Apple Music, and other major streaming platforms, "Flies of Hunger" showcases Melodramatic's constant experimentation and dedication to his artistic endeavors.

Melissa Whiteford St. Clair

Erosion

A firm foundation worn away.
erosion

A gulley cut in the heart led astray.
erosion

Failed communication belay.
erosion

A hopeful spirit crushed by delay.
erosion

Ulterior motives at play.
erosion

Rotten attitudes causing decay.
erosion

A trust factor betrayed.
erosion

A damaging comment conveyed.
erosion

Silt,

sediment,
and sentiment.

Rebuilt.

Founder of White Girl Advocacy, Melissa Whiteford St. Clair found herself emotionally affected by the rise of social injustice in the U.S. She shares her message of unity and social justice through interactive advocacy workshops, antiracism efforts, poetry readings, and talks. Melissa has published two books of poetry "Home Work A Collection of Poems Sparked by One White Woman's Journey on the Matter of Race" and "Heart Work A Heart-Centered Collection of Poems" and "White Girl Homework," a self-guided workbook. She is also a contributing poet to the "South Carolina Bards Anthology 2023."

Halie Stockett

The Man You Are

Each time the water hits the wood
A soft ripple echoes through this tiny shed
a night breeze carries in salty air
gently rocking the rickety boat tied to the dock
Small silhouettes move against the night sky, the bats have awoken
full moon pours across the lake -
sweeps across your somber face
And the stars catch in your eyes as they meet mine
Moonlight always accentuates your features
Your eyes - heavenly, doleful
so dark they nearly match the unruly, raven hair that frames your face
the arch of your nose, gracile lips, the way your eyebrows knit together
Crinkles at every corner - time's gift
My fingertips know each one by heart
As they do your dimpled cheeks
And the scars on your hands.
How exquisite you are
yet is not the physicality of you that I most revere
But the intricate mosaic that resides within
It's you that questions how exceptional you'd be if life had not been so harsh
Had time not traced lines in your skin
And scars not littered your body

How delicate your heart may be
Had love not riddled it with anguish
how much light would pour from your soul
If darkness had not dismantled it
You are not an emotional man
Apathetic, stoic
But you stand before me with tears threatening your facade
The battered boy that augmented this gentle man seeps through
Insecurities stream down your face, stature sulking
Tight lipped, hands tucked in pockets
attempting to conceal yourself from me
To remain unseen, but
I see you

Halie Stockett is a 26 year old Michigan born poet who moved to Charleston to enjoy coastal life. She has been writing since she was in her early teens and hopes to one day reach hearts all over the world with her words. When she is not writing Halie is a full time nanny, concert enthusiast and beach goer. She also spends as much time as she can with friends and family.

HollyAnna Vaughn

i am a poem that never makes it beyond drafts
a messy
chaotic
assortment of words with no meaning

i am a word vomit coping mechanism
the ramblings of a lunatic
who am i who am i who am i
what's the point
who am i

i am caffeine shakes and massive earthquakes and a poem not worth reading
i'm eraser marks
writing in the dark

a poem that never makes it beyond drafts

HollyAnna was born and raised in the small town of Belton, SC. From a very early age, she was drawn to art and creativity. Over the years, her love for creativity shifted towards a love for writing and she is currently in the process of writing her first poetry collection. When she isn't writing or painting in her living room, she is out exploring her beautiful home of Greenville, SC with those she loves most. HollyAnna believes that everyone has a story to tell, and it is through poetry that she will tell hers.

Christine Vernon

A Daughter's Love

In quiet times I remember him,
bright smile and crisp blue eyes.
The thought of him brings my heart to dance
and draws my breath to sighs.
But where has he gone but to another land,
a world I cannot see.
Although I know he's surrounded my soul
in his loving memories.
Someday, I'll follow in his steps
and enter his world of white.
I'll see him there and feel his love,
his smile I miss so bright.
This gentle man now lives with HIM,
he is finally at peace.
He'll take my hand and I'll follow him.
A daughter's love will never cease.

Christine Vernon lives on the South Carolina coast in a small fishing village named Murrells Inlet. Christine is a local storyteller, published author, award-winning poet and artist. She is also the owner of Miss Chris' Inlet Walking Tour- a ghost & history tour she hosts on the Murrells Inlet MarshWalk.

Richard Wainright

Lazy River

The Waccamaw flows through Carolina,
Primitive and indifferent to man.
Unspoiled by the ruin of civility,
Unblemished and undammed.

Water blacker than a psychopath's heart,
In no hurry to get to the sea.
Winding slowly, eventually south,
Tween rice fields and cypress knees.

Countless creatures call it home,.
The lifeblood of existence..
The ecosystem it supports,
The source of their subsistence.

The dawn's light brings renewal
Nocturnal creatures seek shelter.
Darwin did not provide
Protection from the daytime swelter.

An alligator guised as wood
Patrols his private sanctuary
Floating effortlessly, without a sound
Hunting food or adversary.

A sequestered snake, on the bank
Fostered by thorny vines.
Patiently, motionless, lying in wait
For the hapless on which to dine.

Sun-seeking slider turtles
Balanced on a fallen tree.
Basking in the restorative warmth
But always prepared to flee.

High above the river's run
An osprey guards its aerie
Ever watchful o'er her brood
Vigilant and wary.

The water hyacinth floats freely
A blossoming lavender bouquet
Adding contrast and color
To the opaque waterway.

The noontide mood is siesta serene
The water without corrugation
But the movement of any inhabitant
Could cause a deadly confrontation.

A change marks the evening time
When shadows animate.
Night creatures wake up hungry,
Hunting owl's eyes dilate.

Yang turns to yin. Color and hope fade.
The night is primitive and stark,
The alligator works a double shift,
The king of the daylight and the dark.

Turning diurnal to nocturnal,
The setting sun colorfully cools.
From the shadows along the bank,
Eyes Illuminate as deadly jewels.

Richard Wainright is a disabled 20-year veteran, who resides on the intracoastal waterway in Myrtle Beach. He has previously been published in The Archarios LIterary Arts Magazine, Tempo Literary Magazine, and most recently the 2023 South Carolina Bards Poetry Anthology. Richard graduated Summa Cum Laude from Coastal Carolina in 2022 at the age of 70.

Marv Ward

Lonesome Whistle

The mournful bellow of a freight locomotive
singing through the silence of the dawn,
reminds me
that I still live in the South.
And as I roll in my bed,
I can hear the echoes of
Jimmy Rogers' and Hank Williams'
anthems in my head
and I rest easy in the company
of compadres who have eulogized that haunting symphony.

Blues and Americana singer, songwriter and guitarist "Reverend" Marv Ward has performed throughout the United States and shared the stage with some of the most well-known artist in music today.
Ward writes poetry with the same passion that he composes his songs. He has three collections of poetry now published "One Lone Minstrel, "Healing Time," and his latest "Bar Stool Poet", to go along with his six published solo CD's.

Amanda Rachelle Warren

Isolated Thunderstorms/Scattered Rain

The light dims in the kitchen;
                         returns undamaged.
Please let it rain.
The first wave of laden clouds rumbles and does nothing.
Or maybe it is raining, up there. Drops evaporating
before kissing the soft brown of my shoulders.

Everything opens like a mouth, waiting.
Something must suck the stifle from the lungs of this world.
What we want is the clean downpour.
The promise the clouds make in grumble and broil.

Limbo is a leaf unfurling.
Limbo is the seam of the leaf
like the seam of a mouth
waiting to say something important or beautiful, but then only
Come rain. We are all so patiently waiting.

I walk across the room and sweat.
Even my imagined body sweats.
And everything is scrambling for shade.

The squirrels flatten their diseased bellies against the earth,
skinks shuttle from darkness to darkness
in the panting, the wilting, garden.

Amanda Rachelle Warren's work has appeared in *Tusculum Review, The Carolina Quarterly, Appalachian Heritage, Anderbo,* and the *Beloit Poetry Journal* as well as other journals. Their chapbook *Ritual no.3: For the Exorcism of Ghosts*, was published by Stepping Stone Press in 2010. They are the 2017 recipient of the Nickens Poetry Fellowship from the South Carolina Academy of Authors. Their first full-length collection, *Rituals for to Call Down Light,* will be published by Finishing Line Press in July 2024. They teach at the University of South Carolina Aiken with their colleague/partner Roy Seeger.

Riley Willis

The grass, the sky, and the mediator

Her fists suffocated in grass – clenched intimately.
Yet, her shoulders foiled from dirt-troughed nails.
Rested in place ambiguously – With eyes,
stone-thrown towards the sky, and pale hair,
coiled beneath the soil – She wonders:
not as a wanderer of thoughts,
but a journey woman lost – Lest she answers:
a call from the grass to the sky,
through the breeze and fallen leaves – she writes:
a letter in the grass she holds,
common in a bounded feud – all know:
a girl captured by the grass to sky view,
cultivated to be their sower – she lies:
a conversation between the grass, the sky, and the mediator.

Riley Willis is a poet who aims to capture the subtleties of everyday observations onto paper while reflecting on nature, personal sentiments, and the absurd. Riley first had the inspiration to write poetry as a tool to strengthen his memory by recording fleeting moments through verse. His work primarily remains a personal collection, with only a recent interest in sharing publicly.

Leslie Harper Worthington

Cleaning House

Something there is that doesn't love
A Clean House
That fills the sink with dirty dishes
Tosses clothes about the beds and chairs
Scatters leaves and twigs upon the floor
I follow after, picking up
Disinfecting as I go.
Something there is
That wants it this way.
I'd say untidy elves,
But I can't know that for sure.
Maybe it's merely
Consequence of consciousness.
We make messes as we go.
Yet all the while,
There are books to read,
Birds to watch,
And children to sing along.
But nonetheless,
Memory reminds me
of my mother's saying,
"Good habits make clean houses."
And I'm sure they do.
I see her with my mind's eye
washing cup and saucer,

Making beds,
Ironing tablecloths.
She moves in dated darkness,
As it seems to me.

Leslie Harper Worthington is a retired educator who holds a PhD in Southern Literature from Auburn University. Currently, she is enjoying traveling, writing, and spending time with her children and grandchildren.

Toretha Wright

If I Catch A Butterfly

If I catch a butterfly
I will engulf her in my hands
Leaving just enough space for light and air
I will stifle her movement,
Her right to choose
I will forget about her
Until I need to see her beauty
Then, one day, I will set her free
So this other creature will know
How it feels to be plain old me

Toretha Wright lives in South Carolina. She is a noted author of short stories and novels. She also writes and produces other literary works, such as poetry, essays, plays, and short films, which have been presented in many venues. Although her work embraces many genres, her true passion lies in Southern historical fiction.

About the Editor

James P. Wagner (Ishwa) is an editor, publisher, award-winning fiction writer, essayist, historian, actor, comedian, performance poet, and alum twice over (BA & MALS) of Dowling College. He is the publisher for Local Gems Poetry Press and the Senior Founder and President of the Bards Initiative. He is also the founder and Grand Laureate of Bards Against Hunger, a series of poetry readings and anthologies dedicated to gathering food for local pantries that operates in over a dozen states. His most recent individual collection of poetry is *Everyday Alchemy*. He was the Long Island, NY National Beat Poet Laureate from 2017-2019. He was the Walt Whitman Bicentennial Convention Chairman and has taught poetry workshops at the Walt Whitman Birthplace State Historic Site. James has edited over 100 poetry anthologies and hosted book launch events up and down the East Coast. He was named the National Beat Poet Laureate of the United States from 2020-2021. He is the owner/operator of The Dog-Eared Bard's Book Shop in East Northport, New York.

Made in the USA
Middletown, DE
27 July 2024